Coding Made Easy for Kids

Abeer Verma

AF657970

Fusion Books

© Publisher

Publisher	:	**Fusion Books** X-30, Okhla Industrial Area, Phase-II New Delhi-110020
Phone	:	011- 40712200
E-mail	:	wecare@diamondbooks.in
Website	:	www.diamondbooks.in
Edition	:	2026

Author's Note

Hi, I'm Abeer.

I became interested in coding when I started wondering how apps, games, and websites actually work. At first, programming looked intimidating — full of strange symbols and rules. But once I wrote my first simple program and saw it work, something clicked. Coding wasn't magic. It was logic.

What I realized is that coding is really about problem-solving. It teaches you how to think clearly, break problems into steps, and build solutions systematically.

This book is written for students who are curious but unsure where to begin. You don't need advanced mathematics or prior experience to start coding. You only need patience, practice, and curiosity.

I've tried to explain concepts the way I would explain them to a friend — simply, clearly, and practically. Whether you want to build apps, create games, or just understand how technology works, this book is your starting point.

Let's start building.

— Abeer Verma

Grade 11 Student

Preface

Welcome to the world of coding — the language that powers our digital lives.

From the apps on your phone to the websites you visit and the games you play, coding forms the foundation of modern technology. But coding is not just about computers. It's about thinking logically, solving problems, and building ideas step by step.

This book, The Big Book of Coding – Basics & Essentials, is designed to introduce coding in a clear and structured way. It breaks down core concepts like algorithms, programming languages, debugging, and real-world applications into simple explanations supported by relatable examples.

Inspired by India's emphasis on 21st-century skills under NEP 2020, this book encourages students to move beyond being passive users of technology and become active creators.

Each chapter builds progressively — starting from understanding what coding is, moving toward how it works, and finally exploring how it applies in real life.

By the end of this book, you won't just understand coding — you'll feel confident beginning your own coding journey.

Foreword

Technology today is not just changing the world — it is shaping how we think, communicate, and innovate. At the heart of this transformation lies coding.

Coding is no longer a niche skill limited to software engineers. It is becoming a foundational literacy for the digital age. Just as reading and writing empower communication, coding empowers creation.

What makes this book special is its student-centered perspective. Written by a young learner exploring the world of programming himself, it reflects curiosity, clarity, and practical understanding. The explanations are accessible without being oversimplified, and the focus remains on building logical thinking alongside technical knowledge.

This book serves as an important bridge — helping students transition from technology consumers to technology creators.

It is encouraging to see young minds take initiative in demystifying coding for their peers. May this book inspire many more students to explore, experiment, and innovate responsibly.

Contents

Chapter 1

What is Coding?

Story Time

Meet Aarav and Meher, two best friends who love solving puzzles. One day, they visited a science fair where a small robot was dancing, clapping, and even singing!

"Wow! How does it do all this?" Aarav asked.
"It's all because of coding," said the guide. "We give instructions to the robot, and it follows them — just like playing a game with rules!"
From that day, Aarav and Meher wanted to learn this magic called coding.

Explore: What is Coding?

Coding is the language we use to talk to computers and tell them what to do.
It's like giving step-by-step instructions and computers follow them exactly!

Computers cannot think on their own. They need clear, correct commands. That's where coders (like you!) come in.

Just like:

• A recipe tells you how to cook a dish
• A dance routine tells you what step comes next
• A treasure map shows you how to reach the prize

Coding tells a computer what to do, how to do it, and when to do it.

Real-Life Examples of Coding

When you press a button on a remote and the TV turns on — that's coding.
When you play a video game and the character jumps when you press a key — that's coding.
When an app tells you the weather or plays music — that's coding too!

Some Words to Know

Term	**What It Means**
Code	The instructions given to a computer
Program	A set of codes working together
Computer	A machine that follows your coding instructions
Coder	A person who writes code (like YOU!)

Try It: Code Your Friend!

Activity: Human Coding Game

1. Partner up! One person is the Coder, the other is the Robot.

2. The coder gives step-by-step instructions like:

o "Take 2 steps forward"
o "Turn left"

o "Pick up the book"
3. The robot follows exactly what is said.

If the coder forgets a step or says it unclearly, the robot will get confused — just like a computer would!

Think & Reflect

- What would happen if the instructions were not clear?
- Why do you think coding has to be so exact?
- Can you think of something at home that works because of coding?

Let's Revise

✔ Coding is a way to give instructions to computers.
✔ Computers need step-by-step directions to work correctly.
✔ We use code to create games, apps, websites, robots, and more.
✔ Anyone can learn coding — even YOU!

Check Yourself!

Choose the correct answer:

1. What is coding?
a) Drawing pictures
b) Giving instructions to a computer ✔
c) Making sounds

2. Who is a coder?
a) A person who watches cartoons
b) A person who writes computer instructions ✔
c) A robot

3. Which of these is an example of coding?
a) Singing a song

b) Writing steps for a robot to dance ✔
c) Eating an apple

Abeer's Coding Tip

When learning your first programming language, don't try to memorize everything. Focus on understanding how logic flows — input, process, output. Once logic is clear, syntax becomes easier.

Beyond the Book: Real-Life Project

Mini Project: My First Code
1. Write instructions for a simple task at home,

like:

- o "Make a glass of lemonade"
- o "Tie your shoelaces"
- o "Water the plant"

2. Ask a parent or friend to follow your instructions exactly — like a robot.
3. Did everything go right the first time? If not, revise your steps.

This helps you think like a coder — clear, simple, and step-by-step!

Chapter 2

Why Should Kids Learn Coding?

Question Time
What if you could design your own game?
What if you could make a robot move, or teach your toy to talk?
Well, guess what — learning to code can help you do all this and more!
When Diya made her first animation on the computer, she jumped with joy. "I made it move! I told it what to do!" she said excitedly. Diya had just started learning to code — and it opened a world full of imagination and power.

Explore: Why Coding Is Important for You

Coding is not just for computer scientists or tech wizards — it's for everyone, **especially kids like you! Here's why:**

1. It Makes You a Creator, Not Just a User
Instead of just playing games, you can make your own!
Instead of just using apps, you can design new ones.

Coding helps you build things — like websites, stories, animations, and even robots!

2. It Builds Problem-Solving SkillS

Coding teaches you to think step-by-step.
If something doesn't work, you figure out why — and try again.
That's problem-solving!
Just like solving a puzzle or finding a way through a maze, coding helps you learn how to break problems into smaller steps.

3. It Boosts Creativity

With coding, you can create stories with characters, build fun quizzes, or even make music play when you press a button.
It's like digital art and logic coming together!

4. It Connects You to the Future

From self-driving cars to voice assistants like Alexa — coding is all around us.
When you learn coding, you're getting ready for the future!
Future jobs, future inventions, future tools — they all need coding.

5. It Helps in Other Subjects Too

Coding is like a superpower that supports:

- Math (patterns, logic, sequencing)
- English (storytelling in games and apps)
- Art (designing characters and scenes)
- Science (simulations and experiments)

Try It: Design Your Dream Game

Activity: My Game Idea

1. Think of a game you'd love to play.

2. Answer these:

  o What's the name of your game?

- o Who are the main characters?
- o What happens in the game?
- o What would you win?

Now draw it on paper and label the parts. This is how real game makers begin — with ideas!

Think & Reflect

• What would YOU like to build with code?
• Have you ever used an app or website and thought, "I could make this better"?
• How does it feel to be someone who creates things — not just uses them?

Let's Revise

✔ Coding helps you create games, apps, and animations
✔ It improves thinking, problem-solving, and creativity
✔ Coding is useful in school subjects like maths, science, and art
✔ Learning coding today prepares you for tomorrow's world

Check Yourself!

Tick the correct answer:

1. What can you do with coding?
a) Watch cartoons
b) Create your own animation ✔
c) Eat ice cream

2. Coding helps in:
a) Playing only
b) Sleeping more
c) Solving problems and creating things ✔

3. Coding is useful in which subject?

a) Only in computer class

b) Math, art, science and more ✔

c) None

Abeer's Coding Tip

Before writing code, write the solution in plain English. If you can explain your logic clearly on paper, coding it becomes much simpler.

Beyond the Book: Code Your School Project

Mini Project:

My Coding Dream

1. Write about something you wish you could build using code.
    - o A robot friend?
    - o A storytelling app?
    - o A quiz for your classmates?

2. Share your idea with your class or draw it out.

Bonus: Give it a name and explain why it's helpful or fun.

Chapter 3

Meet the Computer

Input, Process, Output

Imagine This…

You press the keys on a piano and music plays. You tap a button on your tablet, and a cartoon starts. But have you ever wondered how the computer knows what to do when you press something?

Coding is like a magic spell — but behind the magic, there's a pattern called Input → Process → Output.

Let's explore how computers follow this pattern!

Explore: The Computer's Way of Thinking

Computers work just like your brain:

1. Input – You see or hear something
2. Process – You think about it
3. Output – You respond or act

1. What is Input?

Input is how a computer receives information.
Think of input as questions or commands you give.

Examples of Inputs:

- Pressing a key on the keyboard
- Clicking the mouse
- Touching the screen
- Speaking into a microphone
- Scanning a barcode

2. What is Processing?

Processing is how the computer thinks and decides what to do. It's the brain of the computer, usually done by the CPU (Central Processing Unit).

(Input + Thinking = Result!)

Example:
You press "Play" → Computer processes it → It opens the video

3. What is Output?

Output is how a computer responds or shows you results.

Examples of Outputs:

- Displaying text or images on screen
- Playing a sound
- Printing a page
- Making a robot move

Putting It Together: I–P–O

Action	Input	Process	Output
Pressing play on music app	Touch	Reads command	Music plays
Typing on keyboard	Keyboard input	Understands letters	Shows text on screen
Asking Alexa a question	Voice	Converts words to meaning	Answers back

Try It: Act Like a Computer!

Activity: I–P–O Role Play

With your friends, act out the parts of a computer:

- **Person 1:** Input (e.g., clap hands, say something)
- **Person 2:** Process (think or "calculate")
- **Person 3:** Output (do something like wave or respond)

Example:
Input: "What's 2 + 2?"
Process: Think and calculate
Output: "4!"

Think & Reflect

- What are the different types of inputs and outputs in your favorite game?
- Why is processing so important between input and output?
- Can you guess what happens when the process doesn't work properly?

Let's Revise

✔ Computers follow a pattern: Input → Process → Output
✔ Input is how we talk to the computer (keys, touch, voice)

✔ Process is how the computer thinks using its CPU
✔ Output is how the computer answers back (screen, sound, print)

Check Yourself!

Fill in the blanks:

1. The part of a computer that shows the result is called the _______.
→ Output ✔
2. When we type on a keyboard, that is an example of _______.
→ Input ✔
3. The CPU helps the computer _______ the instructions.
→ Process ✔

Beyond the Book: Explore I–P–O Around You

Mini Project: Home Hunt for I–P–O
Find 3 things at home that work using Input → Process → Output.

Examples: Washing machine, TV remote, calculator

Draw a simple table like this:

Device	Input	Process	Output
Microwave Oven	Buttons pressed	Sets time and temperature	Heats food
Remote Control	Button click	Signal is sent to the TV	TV changes channel

Bonus: Draw pictures of each item and label the 3 steps!

Chapter 4

Block Coding vs. Text Coding

Imagine This...
Diya wanted to make a cat dance on her computer screen. Aarav said, "You'll have to learn coding!"
"But I don't know how to type code," said Diya.
"No worries," said Aarav. "We'll use block coding. It's like playing with digital LEGO!"
And so they began creating their first game — without typing a single line of code!

Explore: Two Ways to Code

Just like we can speak different languages (Hindi, English, Tamil, etc.), computers can understand code in different forms too.

There are two popular ways kids learn coding:
1. Block Coding – Like Building with Bricks
Block coding uses colorful drag-and-drop blocks that fit together like puzzle pieces.

Each block tells the computer to do something.
Block coding is perfect for beginners!
It's visual, fun, and there's no need to type.

Examples of block coding platforms:
• Scratch
• Code.org
• Tynker
• Blockly

Example:
To make a character move, you might stack these blocks:
• "When clicked"
• "Move 10 steps"
• "Say Hello"

2. Text Coding – Like Writing Sentences

Text coding means typing actual code using a coding language like:
• Python
• HTML
• JavaScript
This is used when you're ready to level up!

Example in Python:
python
CopyEdit
```
print("Hello, world!")
```
It gives you more power and control, but you must type carefully — even one mistake can cause an error.

Block vs Text: A Fun Comparison

Feature	Block Coding	Text Coding
What it looks like	Colorful blocks you drag and drop	Typed lines of words and symbols
Easy to learn?	Yes – Great for beginners	Medium – Needs careful typing
Platforms	Scratch, Blockly	Python, JavaScript
Mistakes	Hard to make	Easy to make spelling/ syntax errors
Creativity	Good for games, animations	Great for apps, websites, robots

Try It: Match the Code!

Activity: Block vs Text
Below are two ways to say the same thing. Match them!

Action	Block Code (in Scratch)	Text Code (in Python)
Say Hello	"Say [Hello] for 2 seconds"	print("Hello")
Move Forward	"Move 10 steps"	move_forward(10) (imaginary)
Start When Clicked	"When flag clicked"	on_start() or def start():

Draw lines to connect the actions to both versions!

Think & Reflect

• Which do you find easier: blocks or text?
• Why do you think we start with block coding first?
• How does block coding help us understand how real code works?

Let's Revise

✔ Block coding uses visual blocks — great for beginners
✔ Text coding uses typed commands — great for advanced projects
✔ Both ways teach logic, sequences, and creativity
✔ You can start with blocks and later move to text — just like learning alphabets before writing sentences

Check Yourself!

Choose the correct answer:

1. Which coding method uses drag-and-drop blocks?
a) Text coding
b) Block coding ✔
c) None

2. Which is harder to make spelling mistakes in?
a) Block coding
b) Text coding ✔
c) Typing homework

3. Scratch is an example of:
a) A food
b) A game
c) A block coding platform ✔

Abeer's Coding Tip

Don't stress about choosing the "best" language. Start with one beginner-friendly language and build confidence. Switching languages later becomes easier once you understand core concepts.

Beyond the Book: Try Scratch!

Mini Project: Make a Character Dance

1. Open scratch.mit.edu
2. Create a free account (with parent or teacher help)
3. Choose a character

4. Add blocks to:

- o Start when clicked
- o Move 10 steps
- o Turn 15 degrees
- o Say "I love coding!"

Decorate your scene and share it with friends!

Chapter 5

Sequences

The Order of Actions

Let's Play Chef!
Imagine you're making a sandwich. What do you do first — put the bread or spread the jam?

If you put jam on nothing, it makes a mess! You need to follow steps in the right order.

That's what coding sequences are all about — doing things in the correct order so the computer knows what to do.

Explore: What Is a Sequence in Coding?

A sequence is a list of steps or instructions that happen one after another.
Just like a recipe or a dance routine!
In coding, each instruction happens in order, from top to bottom.
If you mess up the order — the program might not work right.

Real-World Examples

Task	Steps in Sequence
Brushing your teeth	1. Pick up brush → 2. Add toothpaste → 3. Brush teeth
Getting dressed	1. Pick shirt → 2. Wear pants → 3. Tie shoes
Making a sandwich	1. Take bread → 2. Spread jam → 3. Close sandwich

Now imagine doing them out of order — it won't make sense!

In Coding

Let's say you want your character to jump and then speak.
Correct Sequence:
1. Jump
2. Say "Hello!"

Wrong Sequence:
1. Say "Hello!"
2. Jump

The order changes what the character does — just like in real life!

Try It: Fix the Broken Code!

Activity: Mixed-Up Actions
Here's a scrambled set of steps for brushing your teeth. Rearrange them in the correct order:
- a) Rinse your mouth
- b) Brush your teeth
- c) Pick up your toothbrush
- d) Put toothpaste on it

Your correct sequence:

1. ______________________________
2. ______________________________
3. ______________________________
4. ______________________________

Bonus: Try coding this sequence in Scratch with blocks!

How Computers Use Sequences

When you write code like:

python
CopyEdit
print("Get up")
print("Brush your teeth")
print("Eat breakfast")

The computer follows the instructions in exact order — line by line. If you swap lines, the actions will happen differently!

Example in Block Code (Scratch):

Sequence of Blocks	What Happens
"When clicked → Say 'Hi' → Move 10 steps"	First says Hi, then moves
"Move 10 steps → Say 'Hi'"	First moves, then says Hi

Think & Reflect

- Can you think of something you do every morning that has a sequence?
- What happens when you don't follow the right order?
- Why is it important for computers to follow exact sequences?

Let's Revise

✔ A sequence is a set of actions done in a specific order
✔ In coding, computers follow instructions step by step
✔ If the sequence is wrong, the result might be wrong too
✔ Sequences are everywhere — from recipes to games to school routines

Check Yourself!

Fill in the blanks:
1. A list of steps in the right order is called a _______.
→ Sequence ✔
2. If the steps are not in order, the program might not _______.
→ Work ✔
3. Computers read code from _______ to _______.
→ Top to bottom ✔

Beyond the Book: Sequence Your Day

Mini Project: My Daily Routine
1. Make a chart of your morning routine (in 5 steps).
2. Write or draw each step in the correct order.
3. Now try coding it using simple words or Scratch blocks.

Example:
- Wake up
- Brush teeth
- Eat breakfast
- Pack school bag
- Go to school

Challenge: Can you make a Scratch character follow your routine?

Chapter 6

Loops

Doing Things Again and Again

Let's Count!
"Jump!" said Aarav to his robot.
The robot jumped once.
"Again!" he said. The robot jumped again.
"Five times, please!" Aarav sighed.
What if there was a way to tell the robot: "Jump 5 times!" all at once?
That's where loops come in! They help us repeat actions without writing them over and over again.

Explore: What is a Loop in Coding?

A loop is a special instruction that tells the computer:
"Do this again... and again... and again!"
Instead of writing:
python
CopyEdit
print("Hi")

print(“Hi”)
print(“Hi”)

We can use a loop to write:
python
CopyEdit
for i in range(3):
  print(“Hi”)
And it will say “Hi” three times!

Why Use Loops?

- To save time
- To make code shorter
- To do things in a pattern or rhythm

Real-Life Examples of Loops:

Everyday Task	Repeating Action
Brushing your teeth	Move brush back and forth
Clapping in a song	Clap-clap-clap-clap
Exercising	10 jumping jacks
Drawing a square	Move forward + turn (repeat 4 times)

Loops in Block Coding (Scratch)

In Scratch, a loop block looks like:
- “Repeat 10 times”
- “Forever”

Example:
- “Repeat 4 times → Move 10 steps → Turn right 90°”
→ This will draw a square!

Loops in Text Coding (Python)

Example:
python
CopyEdit
```
for i in range(5):
    print("I love coding!")
```
This loop will print that message 5 times.

Try It: Loop It!

Activity: Loop Dance
Create your own loop dance with your classmates or family!
1. Choose 3 simple actions (like jump, clap, spin).
2. Write them as steps.
3. Now loop them — repeat the whole set 3 times.

Your loop could look like:
• Jump → Clap → Spin (Repeat 3x)
Write your dance steps and test it with a friend!

Think & Reflect

• What are some other things you do over and over again?
• How does using a loop make coding easier?
• What would happen if you forgot to tell the computer how many times to loop?

Let's Revise

✔ Loops are used to repeat actions in coding
✔ They help save time and make code shorter
✔ In Scratch, loops look like "Repeat ___" or "Forever"
✔ In Python, we use for loops or while loops
✔ Loops are everywhere — in music, dance, games, and daily life!

Check Yourself!

Choose the right answer:

1. What is a loop?
a) A way to dance
b) A way to repeat actions ✔
c) A kind of toy

2. Which Scratch block is a loop?
a) Move 10 steps
b) Repeat 5 times ✔
c) Say Hello

3. What does this code do?
python
CopyEdit
```
for i in range(3):
    print("Hello")
```
a) Says Hello once
b) Says Hello three times ✔
c) Says nothing

Abeer's Coding Tip

Errors are not failures — they're clues. When your code doesn't run, read the error message carefully. Most of the time, it's pointing directly to the problem.

Beyond the Book: Draw with Loops

Mini Project: Draw a Shape Using Loops
1. Open scratch.mit.edu
2. Use the following blocks:
   o "Repeat 4 times"

o "Move 50 steps"
o "Turn 90 degrees"
You just coded your sprite to draw a square!

Challenge: Try drawing a triangle or a hexagon using different repeat numbers and turn angles.

Chapter 7

Conditional Statements

Making Smart Decisions

What If...

Imagine you're playing a game:
If you press the red button, you win 10 points.
If not, the game says, "Try again!"
This is called a condition — something that makes your program choose between two or more actions.

Just like how you decide:

- If it's raining → take an umbrella
- If you're hungry → eat something
- Else → play outside

Computers do this too — using conditional statements.

Explore: What Are Conditional Statements?

Conditional statements help computers make decisions.

The basic idea is:
If something is true, then do this. Otherwise, do something else. This is also called if–then–else logic.

Real-Life Examples

Situation	**Condition**	**Result**
It's raining	If raining → Take umbrella	Else → Wear cap
Score is 100 in a game	If score = 100 → Win	Else → Keep playing
Alarm rings	If alarm rings → Wake up	Else → Keep sleeping (oops!)

In Block Coding (Scratch)

A conditional block looks like this:
If <condition> then
    [do something]
Else
    [do something else]

Example:
"If score > 10 → say 'You win!'
Else → say 'Try again!'"

In Text Coding (Python)

python
CopyEdit

```
if score > 10:
   print("You win!")
else:
   print("Try again!")
```

The computer checks the condition: Is the score more than 10?
If yes — you win.
If not — try again.

Try It: Code Your Mood!

Activity: Smart Mood Checker
Write your own "mood checker" using conditional logic.

Fill in your choices:
If I'm feeling (happy) → I will __________
Else → I will __________

Example:
• If I'm happy → I will sing a song
• Else → I will talk to a friend

Challenge: Can you create a Scratch program that says something based on a clicked button or typed answer?

Think & Reflect

• How do you use "if" decisions in your day?
• Why is decision-making important in games and apps?
• What happens if a computer doesn't understand the condition clearly?

Let's Revise

✔ Conditional statements help computers make decisions
✔ They use if–then–else logic
✔ In Scratch, we use blocks like "if… then…"
✔ In Python, we use if, else, and elif
✔ These are used in games, apps, and real-life tasks

Check Yourself!

Tick the correct answer:

1. What does a conditional statement do?
a) Repeats actions
b) Makes decisions ✔
c) Prints pictures

2. Which of these is a condition?
a) Eat food
b) If it's hot, turn on the fan ✔
c) Say Hello

3. What happens if the "if" condition is not true?
a) It crashes
b) It skips the program
c) It follows the "else" part ✔

Beyond the Book: Create a Quiz Game

Mini Project: Yes or No Game
1. Create a quiz in Scratch or with paper and pen
2. Ask simple questions with yes/no answers

3. Use if–else logic to respond:
- If answer is correct → Say "Well done!"
- Else → Say "Oops! Try again."

Add score tracking using variables!

Chapter 8

Variables

Remembering Things in Code

A Box with a Name

Aarav was building a quiz game. He wanted to keep track of the score.

"How do I tell the computer to remember the score?" he asked.

"Easy!" said Diya. "Use a variable — it's like a labeled box that stores your score!"

Just like you write your name on a tiffin box, you give a variable a name so the computer knows what's inside.

Explore: What is a Variable?

A variable is a named container that stores information.

You can think of it as a box with a label:

- The label is the variable's name (like score)
- The thing inside is the value (like 10)

Why Are Variables Useful?

Variables help computers remember things while your program runs — **like:**

- Player scores in a game
- Names entered in a form
- Number of steps a robot takes
- Time passed in a timer

Variables in Block Coding (Scratch)

In Scratch, you can:

- Make a variable (e.g., "score" or "lives")
- **Use blocks like:**
    - o "Set score to 0"
    - o "Change score by 1"
    - o "Show variable"

Example:

When the player clicks the right answer → "Change score by 1"
The score goes up — and the computer remembers it using the variable!

Variables in Text Coding (Python)

In Python, it looks like this:

python
CopyEdit

```
score = 0
score = score + 1
print(score)
```

The variable score is created, increased, and then shown.

Try It: My Personal Box

Activity: What's in Your Variable?
Draw a box and name it after something you want to track (like:
• age
• favorite_color
• coins
• steps_today)
Write a value inside it!

Example:
• Variable Name: coins
• Value: 20
• **Meaning:** "I have 20 coins in my game."
This helps you think like a programmer: store information smartly!

Different Types of Information in Variables

Variables can hold different types of information:

- Numbers (like 100, 5, 0)
- Words/Text (like "Hello" or "Game Over")
- True/False answers (called Boolean values)

Examples:
python
CopyEdit
```
name = "Diya"
score = 10
is_winner = True
```

Think & Reflect

• What things do you track or count in real life?
• Can you think of 3 variables a video game might use?
• What happens if you change the value of a variable?

Let's Revise

✔ A variable is a name used to store a value
✔ Variables help the computer remember things while the program runs
✔ You can set, change, and show variables
✔ Variables are used in games, apps, forms, and timers
✔ They can store numbers, text, or even yes/no answers

Check Yourself!

Choose the correct answer:

1. What is a variable?

a) A rule in a game
b) A place to store information ✔
c) A kind of button

2. What can be stored in a variable?

a) Only colors
b) Any kind of data like numbers or words ✔
c) Only pictures

3. In Scratch, which block helps you increase a score?

a) Move 10 steps
b) Say Hello
c) Change variable by 1 ✔

Beyond the Book: Track Your Steps!

Mini Project: Step Counter Game (Scratch)

1. Create a new Scratch project
2. Make a variable called Steps
3. Each time the character moves, **add:**
   - o "Change Steps by 1"
4. Show the variable on screen

Challenge: Add a condition — If Steps = 20 → say "You win!"

Chapter 9

Functions

Organizing Your Code into Reusable Blocks

Getting Ready for School

Every morning, Diya follows the same steps:

• Brush teeth

• Eat breakfast

• Pack her school bag

Instead of listing all these steps again and again, she calls it: "Get Ready for School"

This is what functions do in coding — they group steps together into a single block that can be used again and again!

Explore: What Is a Function?

A function is a set of instructions grouped together under one name. When you call the function, all those steps happen — just like magic!

Think of a function like a gift box:

• The name on the box = function name

- The things inside = steps or actions
- You can "open" (or call) the box anytime to use what's inside

Real-Life Examples

Real Task	Grouped as Function
Brush → Eat → Pack bag	getReadyForSchool()
Wash hands → Dry → Sanitise	cleanHands()
Clap → Jump → Spin	danceMove()

Functions in Block Coding (Scratch)

In Scratch, we use the "My Blocks" section to create a function.

1. Click "Make a Block"
2. Name it something like greetPlayer
3. **Add blocks under it like:**
    - o "Say Hello!"
    - o "Play sound"
    - o "Start game"

Then, just drag the greetPlayer block wherever you want to use it!

Functions in Text Coding (Python)

In Python, you define a function like this:

python

CopyEdit

```
def greet():
    print("Hello!")
    print("Welcome to the game!")
```

To use it, just call it:

python

CopyEdit
greet()

This makes your code neat, easy to read, and reusable.

Try It: Make a Routine!

Activity: Morning Function

Write your own function for getting ready:
Function name: morningRoutine()

Inside it:
• Wake up
• Brush teeth
• Eat breakfast
• Pack bag

Now call the function whenever you need to describe your routine — just once!
Challenge: Can you draw it like a flowchart?

Why Use Functions?

• Save time — write it once, use it many times
• Keep your code organized
• Make your program easier to read and fix

Think & Reflect

• What steps do you repeat every day that can become a "function"?
• Why is it better to group steps together in one place?
• What would happen if you had to write the same code again and again?

Let's Revise

- ✔ A function is a block of code that does a specific task
- ✔ It can be used again and again without rewriting
- ✔ In Scratch, use "My Blocks" to create a function
- ✔ In Python, use def functionName():
- ✔ Functions make your code clean, smart, and simple

Check Yourself!

Choose the correct answer:

1. What is a function?
a) A type of dance
b) A block of repeatable code ✔
c) A scorekeeper

2. Which is true about functions?
a) They must be written again each time
b) They help repeat actions easily ✔
c) They only work in games

3. In Scratch, where do you make a function?
a) Motion
b) Events
c) My Blocks ✔

Abeer's Coding Tip

Try building small real-world mini projects — like a calculator or quiz game. Applying coding to real tasks makes concepts stick better than just reading theory.

Beyond the Book: Make Your Own Button Function!

Mini Project: Greeting Button (Scratch)
1. Create a new Scratch project
2. Make a block called sayHello

3. Add:
   o "Say Hello!"
   o "Play greeting sound"
4. When the green flag is clicked → call sayHello

Add a fun background and character!

Challenge: Add a second function for saying goodbye.

Chapter 10

Debugging

Finding and Fixing Mistakes

Oops! What Went Wrong?

Diya made a game where the cat should jump when clicked. But nothing happened!

She looked at the code and said, "Oh no! I used 'move 10 steps' instead of 'jump'!"

Just like we make spelling mistakes in writing, we can make errors in our code too.

Finding and fixing these mistakes is called debugging — and it's one of the most important skills in coding.

Explore: What is Debugging?

Debugging is the process of:

1. Spotting errors in your code
2. Understanding what went wrong
3. Fixing it so the code works properly

Think of it as being a detective for your computer — looking for clues and solving problems!

Why is it called "Debugging"?

A long time ago, a real moth (a bug) got stuck in a computer and caused it to crash!
Ever since, any problem in a program is called a "bug" — and fixing it is debugging.

Common Bugs in Block Coding (Scratch)

Bug	What It Means
Block in wrong place	Code doesn't run as expected
Missing block	The program skips a step
Wrong number or message	The output is incorrect
Forgetting to press flag	Code never starts

Common Bugs in Text Coding (Python)

Bug	What It Means
Spelling error	Computer doesn't understand the word
Missing brackets or colons	Program won't run
Wrong order of steps	Code gives wrong result
Using wrong variable name	Program crashes or behaves oddly

Try It: Find the Bugs!

Activity: Debug the Routine
Here's Diya's morning routine written in steps. But something is wrong!
vbnet

CopyEdit
Step 1: Eat breakfast
Step 2: Wear school uniform
Step 3: Wake up
Step 4: Pack school bag
Can you reorder the steps correctly?

Bonus: Try writing it as a Scratch or Python routine — then swap two steps and see what happens!

Tips for Good Debugging

1. Check one thing at a time – Don't try to fix everything at once.
2. Read your code out loud – Sometimes your ears spot mistakes your eyes miss!
3. Test your program often – Run it step by step and observe carefully.
4. Ask a friend for help – Two minds are better than one!
5. Don't panic! – Mistakes are part of learning.

Think & Reflect

• Have you ever made a mistake in writing or homework? How did you fix it?
• Why is it okay to make mistakes while coding?
• What should you do when your program doesn't work?

Let's Revise

✔ Debugging means finding and fixing mistakes in code
✔ Bugs can happen in both block and text coding
✔ Debugging helps us understand our code better
✔ Good coders make mistakes — and learn from them!
✔ Testing, checking, and staying calm help you become a great debugger

Check Yourself!

Choose the correct answer:

1. What is a bug in coding?
a) A flying insect
b) A mistake in your code ✔
c) A game character

2. What is debugging?
a) Starting your computer
b) Making a program pretty
c) Finding and fixing code mistakes ✔

3. What is a helpful way to debug?
a) Close your eyes
b) Read the code aloud ✔
c) Erase everything

Beyond the Book: Become a Bug Hunter!

Mini Project: Create a Broken Program
1. Write a small Scratch program — like a cat walking and saying "Hello!"
2. Now, add 2 mistakes (on purpose!) — **like:**
   o Putting "Say Hello" before the flag is clicked
   o Using "Move 100 steps" when it should be 10
3. Ask a friend to debug your code and fix it

Celebrate with a "Bug Buster" badge when you solve it!

Chapter 11

Let's Build Something

Your First Real Coding Project

Diya's Bright Idea

Diya was excited. She had learned loops, sequences, and variables.
"Now I want to build a game!" she said.
Aarav replied, "Let's make something together — a game where a balloon moves and scores points when it touches stars!"
And that's how they created their first real coding project — all on their own.

Explore: What Is a Coding Project?

A project is a combination of everything you've learned. It could be:

- A game
- A story
- An animation
- A quiz
- A robot control program

It brings together all your coding superpowers:

✔ Sequences
✔ Loops
✔ Conditions
✔ Variables
✔ Functions
✔ Debugging

What Will We Build?

In this chapter, we'll help you build your first game using Scratch.
Project Name: Balloon Popper
Goal: Move a balloon with arrow keys. When it touches a star, score 1 point!

Step-by-Step Guide: Building "Balloon Popper" in Scratch

Step 1: Set Up Your Scratch Project
1. Go to scratch.mit.edu
2. Create a free account (ask a parent or teacher to help)
3. Click "Create" on the top menu

Step 2: Choose Sprites (Characters)
Delete the default cat sprite
Add:
• A balloon (your main character)
• A star (the item you will collect)
You can also add a fun background like a sky or garden.

Step 3: Make the Balloon Move
Use the arrow keys to move the balloon.
Scratch Blocks:
scratch
CopyEdit

When green flag clicked
Forever
  If key right arrow pressed → change x by 10
  If key left arrow pressed → change x by -10
  If key up arrow pressed → change y by 10
  If key down arrow pressed → change y by -10
Now press the green flag and try moving the balloon!

Step 4: Add the Star's Movement

Make the star move randomly to different positions.

Scratch Blocks:

scratch
CopyEdit
When green flag clicked
Forever
  Wait 2 seconds
  Go to random position
Now the star jumps around!

Step 5: Add a Variable for Score

1. Go to Variables tab
2. Click "Make a Variable" → name it Score

Add blocks to increase score when balloon touches the star:

scratch
CopyEdit
If <touching star>
  Change score by 1
  Play sound
Add this inside a forever loop for the balloon sprite.

Step 6: Add Sounds and Celebration

Add:

- "Pop!" sound when star is collected
- A message like "Great Job!" after scoring 10 points

Optional:

```
scratch
CopyEdit
If score = 10
   Say "You Win!"
   Stop all
```

Step 7: Test and Debug

Watch the game carefully.
Check for bugs like:
• Balloon getting stuck
• Score not increasing
• Wrong sprite being used
Fix them one by one — that's debugging!

Step 8: Share Your Project

1. Click "Share" on the top menu
2. Give it a cool name and short description
3. Show it to your teacher, parents, or friends!
You just became a creator!

Try It: Personalize Your Game

Now that you know how to build a basic game, let's make it your own!
Change:
• Sprites (maybe a rocket and stars?)
• Sounds (use space music!)
• Messages ("Zoom! Good Job!")

Try adding:
• Timer
• Different levels
• Obstacles (like clouds or birds)

Think & Reflect

- How did it feel to create something from scratch?
- What challenges did you face during the project?
- What would you add if you made a second version?

Let's Revise

✔ A project is how you put together all your coding knowledge
✔ Use sprites, blocks, variables, and events
✔ Keep testing your code and fixing bugs
✔ Share your project with others to get feedback
✔ You are now a creator, not just a learner!

Check Yourself!

Match the block to what it does:

Scratch Block	What It Does
When green flag clicked	Starts the program
Change score by 1	Adds 1 point
Go to random position	Makes star move randomly
If <touching star> then...	Checks if balloon and star touch
Stop all	Ends the program

Beyond the Book: Your Next Project

Mini Challenge: Build a Quiz Game

1. Ask 3 fun questions
2. Use Scratch's "Ask" and "Answer" blocks
3. Add score if answer is correct
4. Say "Great job!" at the end

This uses:

- Variables
- Conditions
- Sequences
- Inputs

Bonus: Add sound effects and a leaderboard!

Chapter 12

Be a Digital Creator

Coding in Everyday Life and Future Careers

What do you want to be when you grow up?
A teacher? An astronaut? A game developer? A robot builder?
Aarav once thought coding was only for engineers. But when he used Scratch to build a quiz game and got compliments from his friends, he smiled and said, "Maybe I can be a digital creator!"
In this chapter, we'll explore how coding is not just something you learn — it's something you use to create, build, and change the world!

Explore: What is a Digital Creator?

A digital creator is someone who uses technology and creativity to make digital things:

- Games
- Apps
- Websites
- Animations

• Music
• Stories
• Smart devices

And guess what? Coders are digital creators!
When you write a code to make a cat dance or build a quiz that gives points — you're not just learning, you're making something new.

Real-World Examples of Digital Creations

Creation	What It Is	How Coding Helps
Game	Fun interactive play	Controls how the game works
Quiz App	Tests knowledge	Checks answers, adds points
Smart Home Device	Like Alexa or smart bulbs	Reacts to voice and makes decisions
Animated Story	Moving characters, scenes, and voices	Uses loops, sounds, and conditions
Educational Website	A place to learn online	Displays text, pictures, interactive parts
Online Drawing Tool	Digital painting apps	Allows you to draw and color

What Skills Make a Digital Creator?

1. Problem-Solving – Finding smart ways to fix or improve things
2. Creativity – Designing characters, games, and fun experiences
3. Logic – Telling the computer what to do step by step
4. Teamwork – Working with others to build projects
5. Communication – Explaining your ideas clearly

And coding helps you build ALL these skills!

Try It: Create a Dream App Idea

Activity: My Digital Invention
Imagine you could create any app or website. What would it do?

Fill this out:
- Name of your app: _______________
- What problem does it solve? __________________
- What features will it have? ____________________
- What will the user see and do? ________________

Optional: Draw the app screen on paper

Example:
- **App Name:** EcoPal
- **Helps:** Remind people to water plants
- **Features:** Timer, sound alerts, plant tips
- **Coding use:** Countdown loop, text messages, sound output

Explore the Future: What Can You Become?

There are so many careers where you can use your coding knowledge. **Let's meet a few:**

Career	What They Do	How Coding Helps
Game Developer	Build games for mobile, computer, or console	Create logic, movement, graphics
App Developer	Make apps like WhatsApp, YouTube Kids	Write code for interaction
Web Designer	Design fun, helpful websites	Use HTML, CSS, and JavaScript
Animator	Make stories move with art	Use loops, frames, and visual coding

Robotics Engineer	Build and control robots	Write code to make robots act
AI Developer	Teach computers to "think"	Use data, logic, and machine learning
EdTech Creator	Build learning games and apps for students	Mix teaching and technology

The future is wide open — and it's coded!

Coding in Everyday Life

Look around! Coding is everywhere:

- Music players
- Traffic signals
- Video calls
- Soap dispensers
- Microwave ovens
- Shopping apps
- Brain-training games

Almost everything that runs with electricity now involves software — **which is made using code.**
Even farmers use apps coded by programmers to check the weather, plan crops, and use water smartly.

Coding and 21st-Century Skills

NEP 2020 encourages children to grow into thinkers, doers, creators, and problem-solvers.
Here's how coding supports that:

Skill	**How Coding Helps**
Creativity	Make animations, games, and stories

Collaboration	Work in teams to design a project
Critical Thinking	Break big problems into small parts
Digital Literacy	Understand technology and how to use it well
Communication	Share your code and ideas with others
Entrepreneurship	Turn app or game ideas into real products

Think & Reflect

- What's something in your home that runs using code?
- If you could build one thing to help the world, what would it be?
- Which coding career sounds most exciting to you? Why?

Let's Revise

✔ A digital creator is someone who uses tech + creativity to build things

✔ Coding can help build apps, games, websites, robots, and more

✔ You can start today — with Scratch, simple projects, and imagination

✔ Many future careers will use coding: gaming, teaching, design, science, robotics

✔ Coding makes you a thinker, builder, and leader for tomorrow's world

Check Yourself!

Choose the correct answer:

1. What is a digital creator?

a) A music player

b) Someone who builds things using technology ✔

c) A code word

2. Which of these needs code to work?
a) A paper book
b) A wooden chair
c) A mobile game ✔

3. What skill does coding help you build?
a) Memorizing poems
b) Problem-solving ✔
c) Only coloring

4. What does a robotics engineer do?
a) Paint walls
b) Build and program robots ✔
c) Sell plants

Abeer's Coding Tip

Consistency beats speed. Coding 20 minutes daily teaches more than coding 5 hours once a month.

Beyond the Book: My Coding Superpower Poster

Mini Project: Design Your Superpower

Create a "Coding Superpower Poster" that shows:
- What you can do with code
- What problem you want to solve
- The career you dream of

Use pictures, symbols, and words like:
Code | Idea | Robot | Game | Save Earth | Future
Hang your poster in your class or coding club!

Bonus Chapter:

Code in Real Life – Games, Robots, and Apps!

What Do These Have in Common?

- A dancing robot
- A mobile game where you rescue a puppy
- An app that tells you the weather
- A smart light that turns on when you clap

Yes — they all use CODING!
Coding isn't just for computers or classrooms — it's all around us.
Let's explore how it powers the real world!

Explore: Where Do We See Coding?

Coding helps machines, apps, and games work the way we want them to. It's like giving a brain to gadgets!
Let's look at some cool places where coding lives:

1. Games You Play

From Candy Crush to Minecraft to simple puzzle games, every game is made with code.

Code tells the game:

- What happens when you tap
- How characters move
- When to show messages like "You Win!"

Real-World Connection: Game developers use loops, conditions, functions, and variables to build every part of a game.

2. Robots That Move and Think

Some robots clean floors. Some play music. Others can even talk! Robots use sensors to take input, process it, and give output — like we learned earlier.

Example:
Input: Someone claps
Process: Recognize the sound
Output: Robot starts dancing!
Behind all that is — yes — coding!

3. Apps That Help Us

From Google Maps to WhatsApp to calculator apps, everything works because of code.
Each button or swipe you use tells the app to run a program written by a coder.

Example: A weather app uses code to check online data and show:

- Temperature
- Wind speed
- Rain forecast

4. Smart Home Devices

Ever seen lights turn on with a voice command?
That's because of Artificial Intelligence (AI) and code working together.

Examples:
• Alexa, Siri, and Google Assistant
• Smart doorbells
• Voice-controlled fans or TVs

5. Classroom Tools and Learning

Many learning apps like BYJU'S, Khan Academy, or fun math games use code to:
• Give questions
• Check your answers
• Track your score
• Explain the right answers

Try It: Code Around You!

Activity: I Spy Code
Look around your home or school and find 5 things that run on code.

Some ideas:
• TV remote
• Washing machine
• Elevator
• Digital thermometer
• Quiz app

Make a table:

Device/App	What It Does	Where Coding Might Be Used
Washing Machine	Cleans clothes	Controls wash time and spin speed
Calculator App	Solves math problems	Adds, subtracts, multiplies

Game App	Entertains and challenges	Character movements, scoring

Careers That Use Coding

Do you want to:

- Build your own game?
- Make robots smarter?
- Help people learn through fun apps?

Here are some careers that use coding:

Career	What They Do
Game Developer	Create fun and exciting games
App Developer	Make apps for phones and tablets
Web Designer	Build and design websites
Robotics Engineer	Build robots that move and think
AI/ML Programmer	Teach computers how to learn and make choices
Data Scientist	Use code to find patterns in large data sets

You could be one of these in the future!

Think & Reflect

- What's your favorite app or game — and how do you think it works?
- If you could build a robot, what would it do?
- Can you think of a real-world problem you could solve with coding?

Let's Revise

✔ Coding is used in games, apps, robots, and smart devices
✔ It makes technology follow instructions and act smartly
✔ Coders are the people who build, fix, and imagine these systems
You can start learning coding today, and build your own projects!

Check Yourself!

Match the real-world object with its coding use:

Real-World Item	Uses Code To...
Robot Vacuum	Move and clean your floor ✔
Quiz App	Ask questions and check answers ✔
Smart Light	Turn on/off with voice ✔
Calculator	Solve math problems ✔

Beyond the Book: Design Your Own Invention

Mini Project: Code for a Cause

1. Think of a problem you want to solve:

o Help people recycle?
o Remind kids to drink water?
o Teach alphabets with music?

2. Draw or describe your own invention — it could be an app, game, or robot

3. Write:

o What it's called
o What it does
o What coding elements it might need (input, loops, variables, etc.)

You don't have to know how to build it yet just dream it!

Summary Chapter

What We Learned About Coding

Congratulations, young coder!
You've now taken your first big step into the world of coding. But wait — let's take a moment to look back, remember what we learned, and get ready for what's next!
Coding is not just about typing on a computer. It's about thinking smart, solving problems, and creating cool stuff. From building games and apps to controlling robots — coding is your superpower for the digital age.

Explore: Recap of Key Concepts

Let's revisit the 10 coding basics you've mastered in this book!

1 What is Coding?

Coding is telling a computer what to do, step by step.
It's like giving instructions to a robot or writing a recipe.

Why it's cool:
You can build games, apps, and smart gadgets — all with code!

2 Why Should Kids Learn Coding?

Because it helps you:
• Think clearly
• Solve real-life problems
• Be creative
• Prepare for exciting careers
Coding = Future-ready learning!

3 Input → Process → Output (IPO)

Computers work like this:

Step	Example
Input	Press a key
Process	Understand what you want
Output	Show a picture or play a sound

This is the basic model of how machines follow instructions.

4 Block Coding vs. Text Coding

• Block coding (like Scratch): Drag and drop colorful blocks
• Text coding (like Python): Type instructions with code words
Start with blocks. Grow into text.

5 Sequences – The Order of Actions

A sequence is a list of steps in the correct order.
Computers follow steps line by line, so order matters!

6 Loops – Do It Again and Again

Loops help us repeat tasks without writing them again and again.
Example:
"Repeat 4 times → Move 10 steps → Turn 90°" = Draw a square!

7 Conditional Statements – If This, Then That

These help your program make decisions.
Example:
python
CopyEdit
```
if score > 10:
   print("You win!")
else:
   print("Try again!")
```
This helps games, apps, and robots act smart!

8 Variables – Store and Remember Information

Variables are like labeled boxes that store values:
- score = 10
- name = "Aarav"
- isWinner = True

They help computers remember things while programs run.

9 Functions – Reusable Code Blocks

Functions group steps together under one name.
Example:
getReady() might include → Brush, Eat, Pack Bag
Write once, use often = Save time and space!

Debugging – Find and Fix Mistakes

Debugging is finding and fixing bugs in your code.

It helps you:
- Think like a detective
- Improve your problem-solving
- Become a stronger coder!

Review Table: At a Glance

Concept	What It Means	Example
Coding	Giving instructions to a computer	Tell robot to dance
Sequence	Steps in order	Brush → Eat → Pack
Loop	Repeat instructions	Repeat "clap" 3 times
Conditional	Make decisions	If score > 10 → say "You Win!"
Variable	Store information	score = 50
Function	Group steps together	getReady() = Brush + Eat + Pack
Debugging	Fix mistakes	Fix spelling errors in code

Try It: Build Your Own Cheat Sheet!

Activity: My Coding Toolbox
On a chart paper or in your notebook, draw a coding toolbox.
Inside it, list:
- 3 favorite coding terms
- 2 examples you created
- 1 thing you want to build in the future

Decorate it with icons like a robot, laptop, gears, stars

Think & Reflect

- Which coding concept did you enjoy the most? Why?
- What did you find tricky, and how did you solve it?
- What will you build with your new coding knowledge?

Check Yourself!

Choose the best answers:

1. What does a function do?
a) Decorate the code
b) Groups steps together ✔
c) Repeats forever

2. What is debugging?
a) Drawing bugs
b) Fixing code mistakes ✔
c) Breaking the keyboard

3. Why are variables useful?
a) To create games
b) To play sounds
c) To store values like score ✔

Beyond the Book: What's Next?

Now that you know the basics, here's what you can explore next:
- Make your own Scratch projects
- Try simple Python coding on code.org or Replit
- Join a coding club at school
- Explore Arduino kits or robot toys
- Solve puzzles on Tynker or Blockly

Your journey has just begun — and you're already a coder!

Glossary of Coding Words

Algorithm
A step-by-step plan to solve a problem or do a task.
Like a recipe to make a sandwich.

Block Coding
Using colorful blocks to create code by dragging and dropping.
Like digital LEGO used in Scratch.

Code
A set of instructions given to a computer.
It's the language computers understand.

Computer
An electronic machine that follows your instructions to do tasks.
It can show pictures, play music, and solve math too!

Condition
A check that helps the computer decide what to do.
If it's true, do one thing — otherwise, do something else.

Debugging
Finding and fixing mistakes (bugs) in your code.
Like correcting spelling mistakes in a story.

Function
A block of code that does a special task.
Like a box that holds steps you can reuse.

Input
Information or commands given to the computer.
Example: Clicking a mouse or typing on a keyboard.

Loop
Repeating the same steps again and again.
Like clapping hands five times in a row.

Output
What the computer gives back after following your instructions.
It could be sound, pictures, or printed words.

Program
A full set of code that tells the computer how to do something.
Like a game, app, or calculator.

Scratch
A block coding platform where you can make games, stories, and animations.
Fun and easy to use for kids!

Sequence
Doing steps in the correct order.
Like brushing teeth before going to bed.

Text Coding
Typing actual words and symbols to write code.

You said:
summary

ChatGPT said:
Certainly! Here's a concise yet engaging Full Book Summary for The Big Book of Coding – Basics and Essentials, suitable for use in introductions, back-of-book material, or teacher/parent handouts.

Full Book Summary

The Big Book of Coding – Basics and Essentials

The Big Book of Coding – Basics and Essentials is a beginner-friendly coding guide for children in Grades 3–5, designed in alignment with India's NEP 2020 and NCF 2023. Through ten interactive chapters, children are introduced to the world of computer programming in a playful, accessible, and joyful manner.

What This Book Teaches:

Children will learn:

• What coding is and why it's important
• How to use block-based platforms like Scratch
• The key building blocks of programming: sequences, loops, conditionals, variables, and functions
• How to fix errors (debugging) and write smarter code
• How coding is used in games, robots, apps, and real life

Core Topics Covered:

1. What is Coding? – Giving instructions to a computer
2. Why Should Kids Learn Coding? – Building logic, creativity, and

confidence
3. Input, Process, Output – How computers think and respond
4. Block Coding vs Text Coding – From visual blocks to typed commands
5. Sequences – Doing things in the right order
6. Loops – Repeating steps the smart way
7. Conditional Statements – Making decisions with code
8. Variables – Storing and using information
9. Functions – Organizing code into neat reusable blocks
10. Debugging – Finding and fixing mistakes in programs
Bonus Chapter – Real-life coding in games, robots, and apps

How Kids Learn in This Book:

Each chapter follows a child-friendly structure:
- **Let's Begin:** Story or question to spark curiosity
- **Explore:** Simple explanations with examples
- **Try It:** Activities and mini tasks
- **Think & Reflect:** Questions for creative thinking
- **Let's Revise:** Summary of key points
- **Check Yourself:** Fun quizzes
- **Beyond the Book:** Projects and real-world connections

Outcomes:

By the end of the book, children will:
- Understand the logic behind coding
- Gain confidence using basic coding tools
- Be ready to create their own projects using platforms like Scratch
- Think critically, logically, and creatively
- See coding as a fun, useful, and future-ready skill!